Shapes & Colors For Children

Including Hexagon Pentagon Octagon

By Amber Richards

There is a helpful note to parents at the end of this book.

I dedicate this book to my little friend Hudson, who loves circles and ovals more than anyone I know.

Shapes & Colors For Children

Shapes and colors are everywhere, can you look around and see which shapes and colors you can find? Look in the room where you are now, too.

This shape is a circle. The color is blue.

This shape is called an arch. The color is purple.

This shape is a diamond.
The color is peach.

This shape is a heart and the color is red.

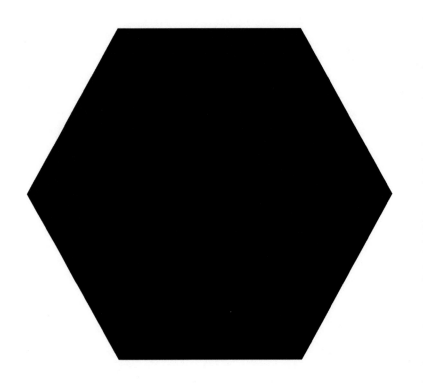

This shape is a hexagon. It has 6 sides. The color is black.

14

This shape is a rectangle, it might stand up and down or sideways, but it's still a rectangle. The color is green.

This shape is a star. The color is aqua.

This shape is called an octagon. It has 8 sides. Can you count them? The color is gray.

This shape is an oval. It might stand up and down or be sideways, but it's an oval either way. The color is navy blue.

This unusual shape is called a parallelogram. The color is brown.

This shape is a square,
and the color is yellow.

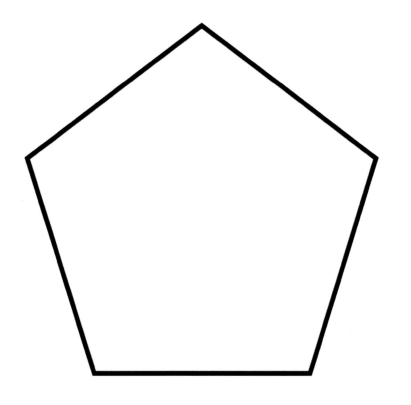

This shape is a pentagon. It has 5 sides. The color inside is white.

This shape is a trapezoid.
The color is pink.

This last shape is a triangle. The color is orange.

The End.

Thanks for reading to the young children in your life. As a mother and grandmother, I found I tended to teach the basic shapes and colors. I'm not sure why I stopped there, but in talking to other parents, it seems like that is a common trend.

When I became a full time nanny, the little boy I cared for loved shapes more than just about anything. Literally, oval was one of his first words. We read, did puzzles and other activities that made learning fun, and he enjoyed every minute, so I kept going in the teaching of shapes.

By 15 months old, he knew ALL the shapes in this book in various mediums. He couldn't say them mind you, but he could accurately, find them, every time. Oval was one of his very first words. I learned a lot from him and how much young children can learn. So don't be nervous about teaching very young children the more advanced shapes, just make it fun.

We would also look for shapes in everyday life and point them out as we found them.

I also found this shape puzzle (http://www.amazon.com/gp/product/B00 0GKATU0) that was very helpful as it brought in the sense of touch, introducing another sensory experience to the learning experience.

Another project parents can do to teach children about shapes is go to a craft store and find either some foam padding, or a sponge, and cut out shapes. Use some tempura paint, and let children use these as stamps, and paint on paper a collage. Fun, messy project that reinforces the lesson.

If you enjoyed this book or received value from it in any way, would you be kind enough to leave a review for this book on Amazon? I would be so grateful. Thank you!

42899270R00024